For the Confederate Dead

FOR THE CONFEDERATE DEAD

Kevin Young

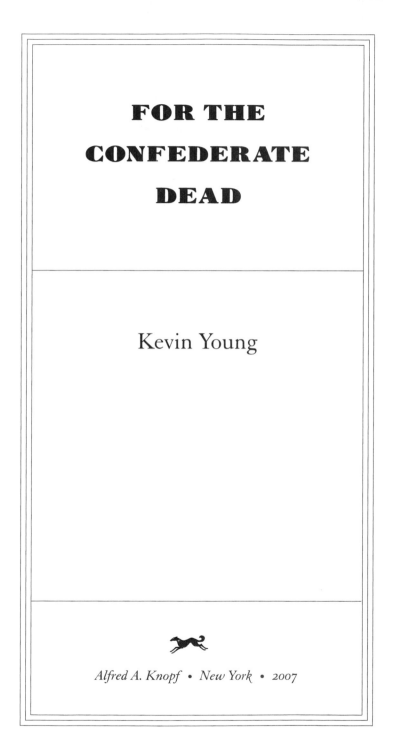

Alfred A. Knopf • New York • 2007

THIS IS A BORZOI BOOK
PUBLISHED BY ALFRED A. KNOPF

www.aaknopf.com

Knopf, Borzoi Books, and the colophon are registered
trademarks of Random House, Inc.

Library of Congress Cataloging-in-Publication Data
Young, Kevin.
For the Confederate dead / Kevin Young.—1st American ed.
p.   cm.
ISBN-13: 978-0-307-26435-0
1. African Americans—Poetry. 2. Southern States—Poetry. I. Title.
PS3575.O798F67 2007
811'.54—dc22   2006047398

Manufactured in the United States of America
First Edition

For Philippe Wamba

1971–2002

This is a beautiful country.

—John Brown,
on his way to the gallows

CONTENTS

ELEGY FOR MISS BROOKS

i.m. Gwendolyn Brooks

1917–2000

There's nothing left
to say. You have done
        your dance, away—
to the place we never thought
    would gather you

    though somewhere we knew
how days grow shorn. Unbrittle,
        brave, graceful yet laceless,
you struck the stone till you were
    the stone, or the face

    each dark rock hides, if only
from itself. Somethin else. The water
        wears over us —
headed home, salt-ward.
    We wade in your wake

    & pray. Forever
bendable, you never did stoop —
        whenever sidewalk's hard heat
met your dandelion wild,
    you fought that white

    head through.
A thankful while, the wind
        our way blew.
Without you, we might not know
    what wind must do—

it too refuses to remain
unseen, keeps many names.
            Gust, bluster, hurricane,
Bronzeville's heavy hawk—
      you swirl & save us

      from standing still,
unsailed. What the devil
            are we without you?
I tuck your voice, laced
      tight, in these brown shoes.

NICODEMUS

Being a true account
of the flight of Freedmen
during Redemption
to the Colored Canaan

"Why do you wear
Your shroud while you are living, Nicodemus?
And a black shroud at that?"

—EDWIN ARLINGTON ROBINSON

Nicodemus was a slave of African birth,
    And was bought for a bag full of gold;
He was reckoned a part of the salt of the earth,
    But he died years ago, very old.
Nicodemus was a prophet, at least he was as wise,
    For he told of the battles to come;
How we trembled with fear, when he rolled up his eyes,
    And we heeded the shake of his thumb.

[FLAME]

Soon as I saw the song I knew,
dropped my plow, unhitched
& headed to where Blue sported
two hoes, hauling much as two men.
Said, "I swear Blue it's so good
we're already gone." I couldn't tell him
what it said, just lured him like a moth
from the hot lamp of the field
& pointed. HO KANSAS! the ad
read, he said, good land, good water
& rocks, good wood on the streams
only $5 a passage. "Nicodemus, now
ain't that name the sweetest heard
since your own?" Finished reading aloud,
Blue just sat in his indigo, sweaty
& shook. No one could cover the country mile
of that man's smile, not even
his gals at them dances, but here
he sat shaking his head till blue
as his shirt & name. Didn't say a word

but didn't need to—we'd been brothers
since Big Massa died & told us so,
called me son, tho don't tell that
to the Widow cause she don't
like to hear what she already know.
Me, I just left Blue there, gathered
Lucy & Moses & the rest to say
what I'd heard. We all knew
of the blood in those parts—
the man Carolina hung & made
sure we'd heard about. No one named
anyone Nat for years—
but now we could go & pioneer

our own brand of unbranded
freedom. No more paddyrollers
& nightraiders, only the same stone
welcome of the land, well looky there
settlements along River Solomon.

Most would have none of it.
Moses said Missus needed us
in the House & cussed
"Don't know who this
Nickledemon is, but I'se sure
bout one thing—he ain't here
or home." I argued with Moses
& reminded everyone of bad butter—
how this South's Redemption
didn't want us, how the town tried
to ghost us out the vote. No chords,
words, only nods in the small crowd,
grown men acting like sheep
scared as sin. "My folks done this
here Dixie since you were only
dix," Blue said, sad. Only Black Tom
stood & said "I want to be alive
not yall, who're dead & don't know it."

[**AIR**]

Freedom what we already had,
only we were too dumb
to say it. Speak up girl, the white
man said, but Lucy'd been mostly
mute since they'd taken our son
from her—Sir, I said, I better
tell her myself, & did. They wouldn't
let us cross with Black Tom's trunk
or her daddy's walking stick—
said she'd have to leave them
ashore, or have them sent. "No" needs
no translation & neither did her
sorrow. They sent the stick & trunk
overboard like so much heavy hay.

We'd made Orleans three days
& camped at the bank. I couldn't
sleep or wait for the Committee
of Colored Folks to meet, awake watched
the water carried out to sea—pitchered
slaves shivering, sold, or shucked
overboard like rotten cobs from Missourah
where they say a colored man can't walk.

Next day the boats left bound
for Kentucky & Kansas, coming from far
as Tennessee & St. Louie just to spot
free soil, call it your own. The Committee
& Colony already paid, all we needed
was what we had: one mule, a year
saved up & some backs & hands
unafraid of work. So we set out
without a thought or second

to waste & my Lucy began
to hum—what I hadn't heard
since she found our son, fetched
me quiet to cut his body down.

[WATER]

Wyandotte, the Kaw, Saint Joe—
the names came to me like stories
my mother told of her daddy
who flew north one night & could write
with both hands. Say he had
bird & no slave in him, say he went
to find his tribe who knew to swim
& sing. Black as Blue was, he had
no nigger's nose, & I suppose
no need for north or Canaan,
Kansas or Canada. He stayed.
I got that bird in me & Lucy

that stubborn black. Black Tom's body
which made it alive most the way here,
all but buried itself—alls I did is dig
a shallow along the Solomon
to stand him down in. Saw the soil,
tasted it, & that was enough. Lucy swayed
into the shallows, teared, drowned
her daddy's spirit stick I swore I'd seen
the men send over. No Liberia here
for her daddy Tom to return to, his body
must find its own precious way.

[EARTH]

That first year heaven
must have hated us, sent
grasshoppers, drought,
then ice & snow that glazed
our one tree, flat-footed light
glaring back. I caught
whatever all I could
along the Solomon; we ate muskrat
& possum & one time deer
which cured us of wanting

to turn tail around.
Few others lasted past frost.
We dug in like the prairie dogs
that scampered in summer,
that, if winter would have trapped,
we would have eaten. By spring
half-starving, sick of each other,
we were studying horizon,
making ready to move on—
& then, all a sudden the snow
warmed & the grass
unflattened, stood up, whistled.

Stalks of sun grew tall
& waved. We dug out like potatoes,
planted. Lucy began to grow
sick, unable to keep anything down
but bread—the staler the better.
I grew thin with worry. Lord,
don't take this one from me.
Then, miracle, she sat up & made
me know—her face—she thought
what fought inside her was a child.

I drank. Walked the fields
with their short shoots & thought
of our boy, gone
like a whistle, like weather, & wished
back the snows. At least I knew
how to wait those out (though
that's probably what got us this mess
the first place). Found

her home by the fire, warming,
& bent to hear our future—
far-off—muffled inside her. I slept
there a long time, it seemed, dreaming
of food, of feeling fuller than I'd ever been
or remembered. By harvest
she was carrying high—a girl—& the crops
were almost in, when she flooded
the floor like the Solomon—

our second was coming so I sent
for Miss Nancy who left the schoolhouse
to deliver. Days of pain, too much
sun—I paced a moat outside the door
my wife would not let me in.
Miss Nancy had her chomping
birthroot, a knife under the bed to cut
down the pain. Our last, lost,
had almost killed her. And me.

When the shouting hours stopped
I really got scared. After forever,
Miss Nancy called me in

to see her, our purple
bundle of yawn, my wife singing
Name a Evie—sweetest,
first words she'd let out in years.

[FIRMAMENT]

Evie grew up tall & straight—
went to school, taught
me to read, to write
them winter nights

when it wasn't harvest
or time to plant.
The boys I kept
away like the crows

by polishing on the porch
my gun. Word
reached us Blue went
into his name. Lucy went

one night, late,
but that's the Lord's

business, not yours. No last
words, she slipped quiet
& never got to see our child
get older & the vote,

marry, move away as the smart
ones always seem to. That
is that. I have kept
this record for Evie so she won't

forget—but mostly
for my son & Black
& my brother Blue & Lucy—
all the dead who can't.

BOOKER T. ABROAD

a travelog
Aug. 28–Oct. 7, 1910

Negroes in South
    outter edges of
    cities. No
    light. Little government.
    No parks, little
    to make life
    attractive. Less
    crime if surroundings
    were more
    sanitary. Drink
    in these improved
    places reduced 50%

America & help
    Europe.

Sunday market
    Cheapest things at
    Smallest Price.
    Wanamakers Negro

Oneness of Language.
    "   " religion
    " climate.
Oneness of Race.

Women in Fields.

Austro-Hungarians
    separated Negro can act.

No talk on trains.

Negro would know every one.

Austro-Hungarians
    like Negro
    love pleasure.

Race competiton.

Industrial & technical
    education in
    Bohemia

Wife is purchased in
    Austro-Hungary.

Religious hatred.
    Different dress.
    Mohamedans—
    7,000 Emigrated.

Permission to speak.

Women.

Women, carrying bricks,
    "   "   water
    "   making mortar.
    "   unloading coal.

    Women get 14 cts in
    factories.
    Have to return some
    to boss, boss
    returns to owner.
    Working people now
    have more than

two rooms, order
& cleanliness.

Separate Schools,
    officer to
    hear speech.

Low wages in city
    due to people leaving
    country.

Women in
    Brick-yard.

Soldiers 2 cts a day

                    *

Bohemian.

Wooden shoes,

    Cows, chickens
    Women 10 & 15 cts
    men 15 & 22 cts
    Board selves,
    1 Room,
    Brick-yard.

Women in Brick-yard.

Children at
    work on farms.

Wooden Shoes.

20 Languages.

*

Can not judge looks of houses.
    3 classes of
    Waiting rooms.

No money consideration
    when Negroes marry.

One woman filling
    wagon in Viena and two
    men by her side.

Women working as section
    hands. Sickness &
    Consumption among women.

Jewish Dairy farm—
    calves, rake, feed,
    manure.

Children not enough
    to eat in Austria.

White Women in Sewer.
    What colored woman does.
    Not public works.
White men standing
white women as bosses.

Food eaten by poor in Europe.

Food of Negro South.

Drinking in Europe of working
    classes as compared with
        Negro.

            *

Naples.

milking cows
    Bakery—
    Shoemakers.
    Man barefooted behind mule
            to wagon.
    Few windows.
    Letter Writers.

Italians & Negro cooks.
    6 & 8 in Room.
    Candles burning.
    One room. No windows.
    Sick boy.

Followed by 50 beggars
    Filth, disorder.
    Picking lice from head.
    Poultry yard in bed room.
    Black smith shop in bed room.
    Donkeys & cattle.
    One quarter of a mile of
            Poverty
    Everybody begging.
    One room 3 x 8 ft one
            family—
    & Shoemaker in front part.

No sunshine enters.

Compared to N.O. Atlanta & N.Y.
Negro seldom begs.
Gambling
Wet, dirt floor,
Sick babies,
goats & sheep.

Lottery tickets.

Crowded with children.
Good natured like Negro.

Meat rarely gotten except on
feast days

7 per cent of Population voters.
Superstitious,
Church life a mere form,
Crawling in dust.

*

Robbers pray to saints.

*

Sicily.

50 per cent charge to farmers
Yet send no *[illegible word]*
Size 2 to 10 acres.

Guns—

to 3 a.m.
    stealing.
    Brigandery & Mafia.

Old fashioned water wells.

Leaving the luxury & beauty Palermo
Poor Parched land.

cutting of animals
miserable hovels to live in.

Dr. Park & Italian Grammar.

Sulphur mines.
    Two mines.
    Good nature,
No tips.
Dinner Bread & celery
    or onion.

Protect women.

Drinking water five miles.

                *

Naples being cleaned.
    Man from W. Va.
    Hell & brim stone.

Down, down, down, into mine,
    man from W. Va.
    All will stop all work to be
    kind to you.

Type writing machine.

Girl weeping over new shoes.

Baby in hammock.

Cemetery
    Wine 2 cts quart
    Gambling
    Cactus fruit for food.
    Classes that emigate
    to America.

Guards to keep people from
    getting salt water.

Negro encoured to produce,
    they not.

        *

Poverty in Catania

Beef Hoof

Child labor
    Treading grapes,
    18 & 40 cts per day for
    11 hours.
    For dinner bread & peppers.
    Meat once a year.

    Ground down by land lords.

    Users of wine
    treading song—

Everybody works
Children & mandolin.
Children & trade.

Horse buggy & Chickens, in
one room.
No windows.
Cooking in St.

Child 7 years decorating bed.
No toilet arrangements use
streets.
Duty on fish
People crushed
man had to leave 6 fish
Boy 7 building boats.

Woman cooking beef tripe.
More skills than Negro.

       *

Man with gun in Sicily.
    Man with hoe must be
reached.

    Decribe in detail houses
and farms near Rome.

       *

Starvation in England.
    England drink and other
nations.
    Others may be poorer but
not so much drink.

*

What the government is
    doing to
help Hungarian farmers

Raising seed potatoes for free
    distribution.
    lends machinery.

    One year gave away
    100,000 fruit trees.
    950,000 apple seedlings
    391,000 pear   "
    163,000 plums
    81,000 cherries—
    Papers & magazines
    Local fruit shows.

    100 market people in
        Budapest.
    sleep on side walk.

Farmers in *mud houses.*

Ignorance of Slaves [Slavs]—
        must
    always be Shoemaker

Slaves oppressed in courts
            &c
    by Hungarians.

Separate racial colleges.

Bare feet in the field.

Farm strikes in Hungary
    & the South.

Hungry improving land,
    trees & horses, but not
    the man furthest down.

Cracow, Austria.
    visits to Salt mines.

*

New lang[u]age
    every time change
    trains.

Negro in South more flexible
than farmers near Crowcow.

Farm village near Crowcow.
    Filth, cows, pigs and
    chickens, in house.
    Dirt floors
    Solemn people,
    cheap gaudy pictures
    American sewing machines
    in houses. Best house
    in town. Women without
    shoes in fields—women
    and girls every where
    at work.

Smiling & hat off.
Dirt and ignorance of farmers.

Sleeping on straw bed in
　　　cottage near Crowcow.

Kosciusko & Negro.

Polanders, a hardy vigrous
　　　race.

　　　　　　*

Peasant cottage,
　　　one room, dirt floor,
　　　straw bed, cow, chickens and
　　　a horse all in one room.
　　　Filth and seeming misery.
　　　In actual house keeping
　　　Negro a head of them, as
　　　to comforts, conveniences
　　　and necessities of life.

　　　Saw purposely the *worst*.

　　　Saving, frugille race,
　　　but poor. High taxes.

No schools teaching poor how
　　　to live as in South.
　　　Coal mines.

No fire & Negro warmed by
　　　heat from cows & Pine Knots.

No books or papers seen in
　　　farm houses of poor in
　　　　　Poland.

Grinding taxation

Negro & Sunday.

Jew can not curl hair in Russia.

Seldom locked Hotel door in
    Sicily.

*

Copehagen.

King & Queen—
    Dr. Eagan had read up
        from Slavery.
    Looks of children.
    People bought
    Wine jugs at Catania.

Change in looks of children.
    Happy Prosperous
    Spoke to 1,500 people.
    Intelligence of farmers—
    men & women—
Denmark has improved—
        land & man.

Books, papers, &c in farm
    houses. Speaking to country
    people. Like trip through
    Macon County.

    Wives & husbands knew me
    as well as my own Race.
    American flags.

Denmark is saving people
before they go to Devil
rather than [after]

Apple slow.

UN CHIEN ANDALOU

Such brilliant barking! The Carnival
of your voice I hear
but cannot bear,
still love. García Lorca, all

of Andalusia knows
your scent—like mercury
you seep everything

In our olives we taste you
In our drinks.

What the dogs must think!
I see them sit
sniff like old men
around

They can smell fear
from anywhere

even a mile away.
This flat red light.

Because of you we do not
weep for the bulls
who each Saturday die

Because of you we sleep
the whole of afternoon.

How the Moors must laugh
lounging in their heaven!

It must be something
like this—courtyards
and cool fountains. Bliss.

The cost of paper
in paradise!

What color the light,
the world, when they shot
you Lorca
let you fall, face
down, into the grave unmarked

This soft
scarred ground.

Let the dogs dig
you up, bear
in their teeth like torches
your bare bones

that against the night glint

THE BALLAD OF JIM CROW

*from the life
& lore of The Killer*

a.k.a.

*Mister Red, Doctor Death,
Professor Limbo,
John Doe & Jim Crow*

[NATIVITY]

Known by four score
& seven names, Jim Crow
was born
with a silver bullet

in his hand. Some say
on a gambling boat,
others say he met the world
at home, in a shotgun

shack. For certain
his left hand clutched
a tin nickel
swallowed by his mother

so the taxman
couldn't touch it.
That boy was all
she had.

The day was grey.
The night dark brown
A twister was spotted
all over town.

Jim's middle name
was None.
His first left blank
for a few hours

till Mr. Crow came home
& called for *Gin*.
No cigars. Birth certificate
an afterthought—

back there then the county
only thought about you
when you were dead.
Or born silver—

unlike Jim, this wooden
spoon in his mouth
the midwife promptly took
& spanked him awake with.

Welcome.

[**TRINITY**]

Jim Crow's first cousin was Rust.

His reddish head followed
Jim everywhere,
turning into his name
everything Rust touched.

Jim's sister was nicknamed Sleep.
Everyone wanted to meet
her, or meet more
of her. She was known to snore

to wake the dead, which
is what Everyone would be if
Jim ever caught on.
On the front porch he shone

his gun like the sun.
For any suitor fool enough
to ask after Sleep
Jim promised a dirt nap

& that's just a start.
Out back he had begun to plant
row after row
of empty graves like cotton holes

waiting to be sown.

[TEMPTATION]

Jim Crow and Rust loved
to pick fights. Hated
picking cotton. Dug
the ladies, though beauty

mostly puzzled the pair, those
few who bothered to notice
the duo's dusty clothes,
their accents thick as country mice.

Rust had a way with machines.
Could make the broken sing
& when he had him a few drinks
did just that. His favorite

sport was thirst,
which only made things worse.
Stuffed on air sandwiches,
hard as tomorrow's bread

& as broke, they'd wander roads
hoping for more. They picked
fights with The Devil
or each other in order

not to have to fight
someone bigger. To impress.
Folks began calling Jim
Killer, and Rust

Rust. Around thin necks
they stuck out only
for each other, they'd cinch
& loosen like a noose the one tie

they shared, never did lose.

[TABERNACLE]

Since they shared the same
monogram, Jim
Crow & Jesus
often found themselves

getting the other's dress shirts
back from the wash.
This was after Jim
had made it big

& could afford such
small luxuries. He
& Jesus mostly met
Sundays in church

where Jesus came for the singing
but stayed for the sermon
& to see whether the preacher
ever got it right.

Jim, you guessed it,
came for the collection plate
& after stayed
for the hot

plates of the Ladies
Auxiliary (no apostrophe).
To one
folks prayed,

the other they obeyed.

[BAPTISM]

Jim's duel with The Devil

was quick as Hell.
The Devil won,
of course, always does,
but afterward taught Jim a trick

or two. How to keep things close
to the vest, to dress
& impress, how to play
dumb, or numb, to play

cards & keeps.
The Devil lived on Such
& Such Street, kept
an office at the crossroads

by a gnarled tree.
SOULS FOR SALE his sign
read in red. His smile
was beautiful—mostly

a partial from a dentist
just outside Houston, near Hell's
third circle. Poor Jim
loved little—his cousin

Rust, sister Sleep
who he watched over
& even prayed for—
Jim felt like an orphan

& meant to make
the world feel it too.
To know his name.
There, There

said The Devil, who hides
a soft side, despite
what they say.
Have a drink on me

pull up a chair
& bend my pointy ear.
Then poured a tall
glass of lye

for bruised Jim to eye.

[ASCENSION]

The sun set
on all his arguments.
At midnight roosters
called out

his name.
Jim Crow crowed
not at all.
The sun set

in its ways.
Heart in a sling.
Jim's neck in a brace
like a bow tie

for his court case.
For insurance sake.
Always on trial,
Jim was—

the State defended
Jim Crow to the death
& always won. Jim had him
a huge green file.

Jim slept with one
eye open,
hand clenching
his daddy's gun.

The sun just set
there like a lazy dog.
The sinking ship
of the eclipse. Jim

spitshining the silver
bullet he was born with.

*

Jim's fingerprints
always found
at the scene—sheriffs
must've carried them

in their belts besides
their billy clubs & star-
shaped badges.
Jim's song was a smack

in the skull—
a dark drum.
The discipline
of a nun.

Only at night did Jim Crow soar
where the Big
Dipper's drinking gourd
dared pour.

From jail Jim's escape
would take a dozen
dark days.
Took one deputy

paid off
to look the other way
& a birthday cake
with a file for filling

Sleep had gone & baked.

*

One day Jim
just up
& flew away.
One day.

After his daring escape
Jim Crow's name would soon
be fame.
Posted all over town

at lunch counters
& water fountains.
Till then we'll
mostly make do

with bootleg dreams,
dusty whisky.
Like a sun
Jim shone

his gun.
Welcome.
Alone, all over town,
the sun set

like a broken bone.

[TRANSFIGURATION]

Jim had never seen
a rat that stood—could
walk on hind legs—
till he hit

The City & it hit
him back. Surprised,
enterprising Jim
decided he'd do in

folks for a fee,
offered up his services
to those in need.
He made no calling cards—

just headed for Mojo
Mikes, pulled up
a rickety seat
& picked a fight.

He was in business
by midnight.
He killed for a price
you see, not pride

or a plea.
It was a job—
he punched in,
collected his pay

& bought him a uniform—
this smooth shark-
skin suit
& one coal tooth.

It was all he could
afford at first,
& besides, he figured
with his jaw clenched

tight, playing
tough, it'd turn
to a diamond
soon enough.

[DESCENT]

Assassins sleep
like babies, deep
& fitful, it's the rest
of us who pace

& pace, undreaming.
Or dreaming what
we haven't done.
Easier to forget

than regret—
Jim knew this,
slept easy
as the money he made

taking out the faithless,
or knocking off
those who thought
for a moment fate

wasn't watching.
Who tried to siphon off
a bit of the bounty,
or sleep with beauty

as if that could last.
It wasn't the cash
Jim Crow was after,
but to put right

what couldn't be,
or hadn't ever been.
His victims
were lucky, patients

really & he
Doctor Red
helping them along.
Their eyes coins already.

Least they went
quick, had a choice—
unlike Rust
who bit it slow

& steady & fading
as his name

Jim dared not dream.

[MAGNIFICAT]

Now that he was rich
Jim Crow didn't
act like it—done
with sharkskin suits

& linen, he learned
to patch his clothes
& count every coin
like a sin. His woolens

worn away like a record
played too much,
the houndstooth warped
like Bessie's broad voice.

Each month he sent
his mother a bundle
though the two
rarely spoke. Enclosed

is a little something
for food, he wrote.
And when Rust went
wherever the dead did

Jim sprung for all
expenses, ordered the best casket
at Bloodworth's Funeral Home.
The dam of his eyes broke

& Jim couldn't go.
Each Sunday
Jim's mother gave over
her take to God

who didn't ask where
the bread came from.
Neither did she.
Still, every once in a moon

his mother bought
herself a church hat
with shoes to match—
not to hide

her face, but frame
its blossom brown
& remind folks
that humility

need not be ugly.
Beneath her hat, its bright
unfading flowers,
Jim's mother lowers

her head & prays.
For her son's soul. For Sleep
to return. For freedom
from this toil

& the red red soil.
It's me,
Lord, Jim's mama said,
bent her hatted head

& clenched like teeth
her hands.
It's me Lord,
she reminded

herself, whose mother
named her America
and whose father was born
a slave

but died free—
which is better
than the other
way round, if you ask me.

GUERNICA

Survivors will be human

—MICHAEL S. HARPER

It's all there in black
and white: someone
has done it again.

We have lynched a man

in a land far-off
like Texas, hog-tied
and -wild

to the back of a car.

There's a word I have been
searching for
in the sand but cannot find.

                *

At five o'clock in the afternoon

we play ball, hard,
in Spanish
until we bruise

No trash
talk, no beautiful
rejections—just these

shots, the smooth
skull of the ball
and that

slant Andalusian light

*

Nearby they are burying
the boy beaten
by the gang—nobody

knows him, everyone

calls the killers by name.
Names. With handcuffs some
manage to hide

their faces like furnaces

failing—first flame, then smoke
and now only cold.

*

It shifts, this light,
its bruised eye shines

above our heads.
Before us the horse,
javelin-tongued, about

to whinny a word—
that wildness in the eyes.
Again, the bull

horning in—how many
has he drug
silent into swamp

or South, whether of States
or Spain?
If it moans

like a man it must
be a man.

*

One day the writer
the painter rose

excused himself from the table
at which he no longer

could sit still.
Still sit.

Bought him a one-way
billet, boarded the train

or the boat bound
for Paris

land of red and blue

*

Dragged awake by midday
light, hunger
sweating my sheets.

We go out into heat. Sit
shaded and peel the shrimp
we will eat, and laugh.

Seafood fresh as a wound.

*

Precious South,
must I save you

or myself?
On the day of the saint

we watch from the terrace
trying not to toss

ourselves over like flowers.
In the arena

the bulls bow, and begin.
Above the roar the victor

will save
the ear, the living leather.

AMERICANA

pl. n. *a collection of things relating
to American history, folklore, or geography*

*It occurs to me that I am America,
I am talking to myself again.*

—ALLEN GINSBERG

EAST JESUS

The South knows ruin & likes it
thataway—the barns becoming
earth again, leaning in—
SAW CHAIN on a sign somewhere
between Boonies & Sticks, pop.
10, now 9, now 11 (the Bloodworth
twins). Here, in East Jesus

the water tower is about half-
empty, the only bar (next county
over) LA TAVERN & TACKLE SHOP
stays full. THE FUTURE
PLANT FOR IT NOW some signs
might say, but we like our trees
fallen, or cut, or bent precarious

above our houses, about to become
fire. Termites & tow trucks & the Sheriff
Dept in which we each are deputies, except
those who ain't, who never will be. The no
good know it, and love that too—
our newspaper's police blotter bulges

with last night's stars, arrests,
their drunken fingers smudged
into night. Sleep it off
& tomorrow's another yesterday—AVOID
SINS TRAGEDY LEARN SATANS
STRATEGY our roadside church
announces whiles we sit & pray & can't

hardly wait to make love or have
that drink, hungering through
the sermon & shouts. Benediction—
handshakes smelling of chicken
served after church—before crossing
the worn-down (ain't this where Sis
was struck dead) tracks, tall with weeds—

BEDLAM

No such thing
as sleep—just the noise
of night, cars kicking

up country roads—
even the silence
shouts. No one raises

glasses or hell—
just kids, well-
behaved, who walk

home old ladies
refusing tips.
No thanks. What

are we coming to?
Passing cars that
wave, people who chat

and don't mind if the neighbor's
dog dirties the lawn.
Oh well. Everyone

sleeps with everyone
or alone, I cannot
tell. The postman

delivers children
who look
like no one

& bills arrive already
paid. We work all night
at the unhappiness plant

where no one gets laid
off, pull down
a decent wage.

There's no one left
to blame—all the goats
have escaped

to the woods, the wilds
filled with soggy
shallow graves.

WEST HELL

Sin, thy name is this
wait—this place—
a long ways from Here
to There, from somewhere

last we were
in love, or lust, or not
even close. It's hot
most the year

& noon this town shuts
doors, down, the bass
burrowing in the bot-
tom—even our mudfish

with nowheres to go.
The days dry as envy,
we trawl the shallows
& perfect our lies—

the morning's catch we could
have landed, the ladies
or mens, jealousies
we wear as badge, avoid

not at all. How humid
the heart, its messy
rooms! We eat spicy
food, sweat like wood

& smolder like the coal
mine that caught fire
decades ago, yet still smokes
more than my great-uncle

who will not quit—
or go out—

BANESBOROUGH

The Werewolf family moved
next door without a word
or wave. The situation, hairy,

scared me—once a month
the men bloating, became
unhinged. Wired

as their cars for sound, Howling
Wolf on the stereo, wailing
they rode around. From my window

you can see the women at
a loss, pacing between
cracks in the blinds—

under moonlight they fret
for where their sons,
husbands be at

come payday—downtown,
woofing, drinking four weeks
of work away, their beards

grown in beyond regulation, hair wild
as their lawns & tall as The Plant—
poisonous flytrap—that keeps threatening

to shut on down.

OLD EXIT 9

sells Fireworks & Karate Supplies
is now Exit 29
is handy with a knife
wants what it wants
    when it wants it.

Old Exit 9 owes you one.
Likes to dance; doesn't much.

Old Exit 9 forgets
    a joke halfway through
Prefers toast burnt
Is late, Sorry, Can't Talk,
    will call you later
Figures, what the hell,
    let's move in together,
    might as well.

Old Exit 9 plants a cross
where the last accident was.

Old Exit 9 is low on cash,
likes nothing better
    than a waxed moustache.

Old Exit 9 grew up poor
so only likes new stuff from the store.

Old Exit 9 loves summer
& snow both.

Old Exit 9 gave peace a chance
Old Exit 9 has no regrets
Thinks Cleveland's exotic
    & Akron's next

Old Exit 9 doesn't mind
    opening up
    a can of whupass,
    help yourself.

Old Exit 9 Ran for sheriff against a dead man
    & lost.

Old Exit 9 needs
    a babysitter for the prom.
May show up late but visits
    when it can.

Old Exit 9 can't stand
    theater but loves drama—
Has been there
    but not done that.
Is gone, like Mama,
    bless her heart,
    & ain't comin back

HOTEL PURGATORIO

We believe in between,
live with sheets
not quite clean

We are what we leave

The smoke of who came
here before us, who went
after breathing another's breath

Things we cannot see

Nothing on the TV—
We are the channels
changing, chained

to dresser drawers full
of maps to the missing
Legends

which don't much measure

Still, when we drift & sleep
we dream of dolphins—
their slick bodies

buoyant & upright
while walking down First
and Grant

Their click talk
quick as a cabbie's.

Red-eyed, waking,
we drive north toward
Bland and Bluefield

And there! a second sun
alongside the road—

prisoners picking up
trash in their blinding

bright orange uniforms

SIGNS

Does the road you're on
lead you to me?
        —God

⁕

Dixieland
Weekly Rates

The Alamo

⁕

Drive-In
Something   Mary
Armageddon

⁕

PRODUCE

⁕

He Who Takes the Son
Gets It All

⁕

Young's Pawn
& Gun

⁕

FREE TRIP TO HEAVEN
DETAILS INSIDE

*

FAX IT HERE
COLLARDS

*

It's hard to fall
when you are already
on your knees

*

UNITY
1.79 / 17.89

*

Red Star
Fireworks Peaches

*

GAL SK MLK

*

Pray for Our World

Introducing Stylist
Janice Wood

*

DIRT FOR SALE

*

Our Beer's
The Coldest Around

*

Your Hands Are
The Only Hands God Has

*

THROW PILLARS

*

Fragments
Wool Suit Crepe
699

Try God

*

UNRECONSTRUCTED

*

If You Can't See
My Mirrors
I Can't See You

*

When Hell Freezes Over
I'll Climb
There Too

PRAYER

Today even the cows are tired
have lain down, tuckered, tucking
their legs beneath them

in prayer. Their thick restless
tongues, tails, their blank
bovine bows.

No wonder we worship cows.

No wonder we let them lick
the salt from our arms.
Or bend beneath them

& borrow their motherhood
make it our own. Have you ever
tasted fresh-pulled milk, slightly

warm? It tastes of whatever
grass you have fed them: blue
or bitter crab. Mint. No wonder

we swallow cows & save
their skins, find out if we fit.

AMERICANA

America, you won't obey.
You won't hunt
or heel or stay.

America, you won't do
anything I want you to.
(To tell the truth,
I like that about you.)

You're too much.

What mountains you are
America! What minefields
and mysteries, symptoms
and cinemas and symphonies
and cemeteries!

Bully, albino, my
lopsided love—

America, I can't leave you
well enough alone.

America, you've lost
your way home—

I have saluted
your dying woods, called to
your flags trimmed on tin.

America, I am letting you in.
America, where you been?

I have seen your tiny twilit eyes
    your mouth still
    stuffed with straw.
I have driven your bent unbroken
    back and fallen
    to my knees like a nun

    in her black habit
praying you would change.

Today the road runs straight

Today the grey
is yours! the fog
and the burning leaves.

Today the crows refuse
to get out the way

Today I drive the rains
of your rough face
    your citified plains—

America, won't you take
    your hands of hurt away?
    tuck them drawer-deep
    like the good
    silver of grandmothers?

(I have inherited, America, only
    rusty knees, a voice
hoarse from hollering.)

America I have counted
    all the china and none
    is missing.

America, I love most your rust,
    the signs that misspell doom—

And why not your yards
    of bottle trees and cars?

And why not the heart
    transplants we want?

America, tell the maples
    to quit all this leaving.

Warranty up, trial basis,
    thirty days free—

America I have seen
    men whose faces are flags
    bloodied and blue with talk

seen the churches keep
    like crosses burning

seen the lady who lines
    your huddled shore, her hand
    rifle-raised,
    her back turned away.

BORROWED COUNTRY

In the borrowed country
house of her mother
we drink too much,
whine, fuck
not enough & claim
to be lazy

though we wake early
with the chickens
a neighbor pretends to raise
for food. We stuff
ourselves, then head
for the deep end. I am far

from what my grandmother
ever saw of this land
of the lariat, from hard work
& the peach tree she'd send each
of my uncles, my mother,
to pluck their own punishment

from. Here there is no Lent
only Easter break, colored
eggs but no people. Strangers
are polite when we go out—
which is rare—what else
beside us is there? Such thick

undergrowth! Socks
pulled up to our knees like schoolgirls
we wade the backyard. In a voice,
her mother's, I've never before heard
she warns *Remember*
the ticks, beware the chiggers—

INCIDENT

for Mr. David King
who drove me all over Old Baltimore

People think this
        is the last city
in the South, first
        North, but really
North starts up at your Mason-

Dixon. Back then Baltimore had
        the racial discrimination—
but you're too young to recollect.
        Not that there were laws
and court, so-so, or we couldn't ride
        back of streetcars—

you just couldn't cross
        Such & Such Street.
We'd come over here
        pick peach and strawberries
and soon as we carried
        them back, whites
would make us drop
        them sweet bushels
and run. [Laughter.]

I say I'm a mathematician
        cause I'd count and know
how much steel percentage had to go
        to the suppliers—had seven
white boys under me and still

wanted me to walk all over creation
        to go to the commode.
Not me. If someone said a word I'd draw
        my knife and cause commotion—
that'd be the end of that.

Whenever a group of us coloreds
        would be gathered, you know,
talking, all it'd take is two, three cops
        to come along and sound
us down. The others ran—
        I'd stand my ground—

One'd take his stick
        and jab me in my stomach.
I'd call him a *son of a b*
        all while he was hitting me.

[Silence.]
        That fence
wasn't there then. Only time
        you'd see us
over here was to caddy.
        If you were lucky

who you was driving let you
        go to the Chaffeur's Ball—
the womens would get dolled
        up, you know, and we'd go down
to the DC—it wasn't what you did
        but who you drove got you in.

Back there then
        what they call your Inner
Harbor was trouble—
        we named it Hobo Jungle.
Blacks Jews Italians Puerto Rican
        Whites—we all communicated there—

And the fish, you never seen
        so many! [Laughs]
On the docks they flopped and fought
        strong as the smell—caught
in nets or photographs—
        strung up between
two, three men.

SPRINGTIME COMES TO THE CAPITOL

Easter, 1939

The Revolution's Step-Daughters
        will not let
Marion Anderson clear
        her brown throat

onstage, among the blinding lights
        of Constitution Hall—
it will take a First Lady to invite
        Anderson to thrill

a throng at Lincoln's stone feet.
        (In the wings, Anderson trills
the *me-me-me-me-me*
        of practice drills.)

Like sky her throat is clear.
        Everywhere,
folks stop to hear her
        voice's bright thunder—

Git on board, little chillen
        Dere's room for many—mo'—
bringing springtime to the streets
        Benjamin Banneker helped sow:

The podium a bouquet
        of microphones—

This bloom that begins
        all along the spine.

THRONE OF THE THIRD HEAVEN
OF THE NATIONS MILLENNIUM
GENERAL ASSEMBLY

James Hampton, self-taught artist

Evenings I return with my head
Soaked with stars—place
A crown crafted of foil
On my head and set to work

By day I sweep the school
Nights I piece together heaven
The way God intended:
By hand, by saving
What some would throw away

No one sees scraps are what saves

What do I know of purgatory?
Except the cans that once a week
Congregate along the curb, waiting
To be delivered

Some of what I need I find
Among those rusty lids, past peels
And maggots
The metal gleaming

What we gather, we are

When I die and make
My way to that third place
The land-
Lord will discover this

Altar above my garage
Decide it art
Find the faith my hands wound
Each day like a watch
My magpiety

PARADISE GARDENS

The horse-scent of happiness
The long drive west
Or north, past
Our past, ghost towns and glory
Small gods of the fields
That have fed us
And held up our bodies
In battle, that have buried us

When we at last reach
Paradise, it is smaller, and dirtier
Than we expect

All our maps put us quite closer
All day we have driven
Even called ahead to keep
Reverend Finster late
Now only dusk greets us
Paradise shut for the day

Evening and its statues
And fences keep us out

We manage a few snapshots beside
Angels drawn Egyptian
Flat and brown
It has grown too dark to turn back
To wind these townships without
Names, braving the crosses both
Railroad and church

We check ourselves into
The hotel as if an asylum
Cough nervously hoping
The quiet will let us sleep
This county dry but we drink
Canadian Mist someone brought which coats
Our tongues, the ones we speak in
Becoming again young

Pratfalls and close calls
Cartoon the room

The animals all talk
Who die over and
Over again on television—their thousand
Foot fall—the poof of dust—
Still somehow surprises us
Each time they stretch
And stand themselves up

By morning the light
Leans a little

We do not have time to try
Paradise again, to buy
Whatever mementos are sold there
Instead we borrow the Bible
That weighted our bedside table
Reading aloud while we take,
Along roads that lead
From Rome, a faster highway home

Past low houses and rows
Of whatever is grown
The children's swingset
All rust, the gangrene pools
Gathering rain
The small gods of fields
That we have fed
From, blessed, that sometimes a farmer

Must burn in order to save

FOR THE CONFEDERATE DEAD

I go with the team also. —WHITMAN

These are the last days
my television says. Tornadoes, more
rain, overcast, a chance

of sun but I do not
trust weathermen,
never have. In my fridge only

the milk makes sense—
expires. No one, much less
my parents, can tell me why

my middle name is Lowell,
and from my table
across from the Confederate

Monument to the dead (that pale
finger bone) a plaque
declares war—not Civil,

or Between
the States, but for Southern
Independence. In this café, below sea-

and eye-level a mural runs
the wall, flaking, a plantation
scene most do not see—

it's too much
around the knees, heighth
of a child. In its fields Negroes bend

to pick the endless white.
In livery a few drive carriages
like slaves, whipping the horses, faces

blank and peeling. The old hotel
lobby this once was no longer
welcomes guests—maroon ledger,

bellboys gone but
for this. Like an inheritance
the owner found it

stripping hundred years
(at least) of paint
and plaster. More leaves each day.

In my movie there are no
horses, no heroes,
only draftees fleeing

into the pines, some few
who survive, gravely
wounded, lying

burrowed beneath the dead—
silent until the enemy
bayonets what is believed

to be the last
of the breathing. It is getting later.
We prepare

for wars no longer
there. The weather
inevitable, unusual—

more this time of year
than anyone ever seed. The earth
shudders, the air—

if I did not know
better, I would think
we were living all along

a fault. How late
it has gotten . . .
Forget the weatherman

whose maps move, blink,
but stay crossed
with lines none has seen. Race

instead against the almost
rain, digging beside the monument
(that giant anchor)

till we strike
water, sweat
fighting the sleepwalking air.

LOST LOOKING FOR BEHAVIOR
CEMETERY, SAPELO ISLAND, GEORGIA

You would expect silence
or at least reverence
instead there's only noise—

the guiltless birds—
barking—our grease-
free squeaky bikes—

We are like
the light lost. We circle
Sapelo with the buzzards

overhead patient
patient. Outsiders,
newcomers, we are

the night and its armadillos—
fellow non-natives who swam
across the strait to reach

this shore. Last night, beachside,
the stars skywide
and so thick no one could find

Orion or his belt. (The shooting
star I did not see
but believed.) When finally

we find Behavior Cemetery
Rest in Peace
it is almost evening

among the slanted
stones—
        Deacons
and Sis. and Bro.—

        We walk
beside Grovners—
Ceaser, Sr. and Glasco
WAS 72YERS OLD
beside words wind has tried
hard to erase—

ASLeep IN JESUS
    LcSSed sLeeP —

The cracked cat,
ceramic, sits at the foot
of a headstone, its words
        handcarved—
            halting—

GEORGE STEVE
BOrN Mar. 10
Died MaY 28
    ONe bUT NO
        TEN

The cracked reprieve
of graves—

        The newly buried
telephone cable—

The only quiet what I ride
back alone—

                            something
scattering in the bush—

a dog guarding the dirt road
as if it led to the Pharoah
entombed. Tomorrow

the ferry that bears
us back will feel
like our time—borrowed—

too slow—and the water will not
spark into stars—phosphorescent—
as it did, last night, when I

knelt to touch it.

GUINEA GALL

And one day, when, I will cross
Great Water, walk and reach
that final rise

to find them
singing. There,
in the valley, they all will be.

Forgive me, Grandfather, for wanting
to hear you again
for leaning close to strain

to understand what you are saying.
And Mother, Father, for expecting
to kiss again your wide hands

even though I still can.
In my breast
pocket I shall keep

the ticket the conductor
sold me
stamped One Way.

That day even rain can't delay.

And we will sit and rock
and sip our sweating drinks—
watching the sun toward us bring

red light like an arriving train.

APRIL IN PARIS

*Lionel Hampton's Last Weekend
in Concert at the Hotel Meridien, Paris,
Good Friday, 1999*

The light dim
as they bring him—
    Ladies & Gentleman
Mademoiselles & Monsieurs

    Lionel Hampton!—in—
His cane quick turns
    to a xylophone wand—
Dad says the man used to hold

    two at a time—strikes
notes clear as a river
    or its gold.
Motherlode. He's slowed

    some, plenty—
like M'Dear, 102, who
    one night fell off
the porch she thought

    a bathroom, then lay till dawn
leg broken—her last
    and his. (Still, sometimes
you gotta make a break

    for it, like the time
they found M'Dear, eleven then,
    along the highway
with baby brother

having decided to walk
back to their old, all-black home
in Bouley, Oklahoma
where a sign in town proclaimed

WHITES NOT ALLOWED
PAST SUNDOWN.)
Playing the subtleties
of silence, Hampton traces,
like a government agency,

the vibes—quietly—
his wands a magic,
a makeshift. Arthritic solos

hover like a bee
above the flower, finding
the sweet center.
Two days before Easter, Monsieur

Hampton plays the changes,
offering up
songs read off
a napkin bruised with lyrics:

*What did I do
to be so black & blue?*
his voice wobbles
along the highway

called history,
flying home. Here.
(Leaves out the part
I'm white—inside—

because he's not.)
The band, tight, will swarm
        behind & save him
if he falls—when—

        The sax player stops
between tunes to dab
        a handkerchief at the drool
gathering his chin.

        Such
care. The mind's blind
        alleys we wander down.
This is enough, just—

        This is Paris—

In the Rosa Parks section,
        as the drummer we met
before the second set
        dubbed it, we stand

        in the back
& applaud
        & shout *yeah*
& block no one.

        And I say to myself
What a wonderful world—

        Dad's so excited
he falls off
        the risers—& he laughs
& we laugh—

Skies are blue
Clouds are white

Sacred dark light

In which, after, they lead him out.

AFRICAN ELEGY

One good thing about music
When it hits you feel no pain

— BOB MARLEY

POSTSCRIPTS

The world is a widow.

Storms surround us, areas
of low

& high pressure
moving through—

should be gone tomorrow.

Rain from the sky
like planes.

We pull ourselves up
from bed
or death, wander

streets like ghosts,
lost guests.
Everyone's a town

with the shops shutting
down, no hours
posted. Even the radio

stays closed—only news
or fools still

believing love.
Traffic that won't move.

In the crossing, a white hearse
hanging a left.

I want to be that woman
just ahead, tapping her foot
out a car window, bare,

in time to a music
I can't quite hear.

September 2001

SKYSCRAPER ODE

I have seen you rise
& fall like breath, a body
sleeping beside me.

I have seen the buildings rise
almost overnight,
workers like proud fathers
walking the labyrinth of what
your skeleton will become

your bones still
without skin.

Soon each square window
a mirror.

I have seen you
rise & fall like the hummingbird

I found in my garage
who would not go out,
or could not, plunging
against glass

then landing on the sill,
face pressed so flat
I wasn't sure it knew

how to breathe.
Or leave. I couldn't
help it along.

I couldn't help it see

all it needed
was to turn around

& for once I thought
the banker's boxes I'd saved
just in case, emptied,
might be worth some shelter

& I eased him in one
& out.

I know science says
hummingbirds shouldn't be
able to fly.

But I have seen the tall
buildings rise

like he did, a blue
gleam finally, again,
in the light—

flying with the sun,
shining green—

now gone.

11 September 2002

AFRICAN ELEGY
(MUCH THINGS TO SAY)

i.m. Philippe Wamba
1971–2002

THE NEWS [STOP THAT TRAIN]

When you died I was reading Whitman
    aloud.
While you died I was miles away,
      thousands of deserts and oceans
      and mountains and plain.
When you went I was reading aloud the end
      to a crowd trying
      to remember how grief once felt,
      wanting to forget,
      wanting not to.
While you went about that dangerous road
      on your way was it to the sea
I was saying *Look for me*
    under your bootsoles.
Caked with mud.
Caked with mud the color
      of blood, the picture much
      later I saw of your truck
      totaled, towed
      by what was left
      of the axles—
Your passenger brother's breath a miracle.
When you died I was reading aloud
      for the dead, for what
      I had almost believed
      and then the world went
And did this. I cannot forgive
      this world, its gear's unsteady turn,
      that day's sun that shone
While you died trying to get home.

11 September 2002

FADE [THREE LITTLE BIRDS]

I am sick to death
of heaven, of hoping
it's where you are

& your brother long
ago gone What I'd give
to have you breathing

for your laugh & large hand
slapping mine hello—
What up—my name

a throaty thing, a song.
I'm cross with God
who goes on sleeping—

What I'd give to have
you here & hear you sing
every other verse

of Something
in the Way or Breathe
And Stop or whatever else you know

half by heart. Come back
& blast your headphones
so loud I can't sleep

on the train dragging Spain
sing slow again in whatever
tongue you want keep

me awake while we railroad
Europe walk Paris reading
menus off every window

in town before settling
for a hunk of cheese old bread
cheap wine on the steps

of some cathedral we'll never
go in. Back then we'd get grievously
drunk & wander laughing

Now drunk with grief
I'm again hungry
& hate that you are dead.

I hate that I'm still
hungry while you're still—
hate that I can't make

the long flight to see you
not sleeping—my passport
we bought together

a decade ago now outdated
& even if it wasn't
not sure I could see

you expired like milk
my stomach can't take.
Come back—

I meant it that last time
when I said I'd see you
soon, wanted to visit you fat

& happy, well maybe
just happy as everyone agrees
at last you were.

Somewhere I'm sure
you are clipping
your dead brother's hair—

it must be long now.
You were the only one
shocked even hurt when I cut

my locks
even if long since
you'd shaved yours

you said at least I
was keeping the faith.
My hair now

like belief shorn.
Is it too much to ask
the wind to end? If only

you'd say
you'd stay, drink
out the side

of your mouth your teeth
a bottle opener
your laugh much music.

Come back. I'll sell
you cigarettes one at a time
the way they did in Kingstontown

We can clip each other's hair
like we did across Spain & London
You giving me a line

A fade we called it then

Now, tomorrow too, you are
this buzzing behind my ears
I bow my head to

16 September

IMMUNIZATIONS [LIVELY UP YOURSELF]

It is late when we decide
    the long flight to you, to find
    repellent enough to keep
    even this away.
It is late when I think I cannot make it
    and am afraid—
    I can't, my passport
    is old, the picture
    I took to tour Europe
    with you barely looks
    like me now, and yours
    I can no more remember.
It is early when I go
    get the shots to keep
    me well—you understand
    they give you a little
    now to let it
    later not kill you.
There's no immunity
    against grief—
There's nothing that keeps
    away dengue fever
    or a hundred other
    harms—
Boil or tablet the water.
Another pill to take
    the taste out.
Are you ok without menningitis?
I am ok I think I leave
    then go back and get more
    to make my arm sore.
This one lasts you
    for life
This one lasts four months

This one take
　　every day while there
　　and seven days after.
This one you don't need
This one won't take effect
　　till you return.

Perhaps grief itself
　　is inoculation against
　　it all, faith
　　is much of it—
I half forget
　　and hug myself
　　and there it is again—
　　the pain—
For you my arms ache for days.

THE FUNERAL ROAD [BABYLON BY BUS]

Honey's Fashions
on road to the family home

white mannequins
in the window
selling something I can't see

       *

last night when we landed
in Dar es Salaam the smell everywhere
of fireworks in the air

as if something nearby exploded

and no one in the road

       *

Que's Cyber Café on the way
to funeral

right side of his face/fallen

hearse a small bus with a siren

I'll follow him
forever

       *

dozens of blondwood beds
frames empty

Asante Yehova
on a billboard

Thank You Jehovah
For Answering Our Prayers

*

a rooster walking
under a vanity
its oblong mirror

*

Survey Motel
self contained rooms

photocopy binding

*

red dirt in a pile
high enough
for a hundred graves

*

Relatives & Freinds
misspelled on our bus

*

along the long
road to the chapel
one boy saluting

another aiming
his elbow at us
and shooting

20 September

BURIAL [NO WOMAN NO CRY]

We circle the grave
in dark coats like buzzards.
The men, me too, this morning
had lifted you, steering

your wooden ship through
metal doors to the living room.
I couldn't stand to see
the screws still loose.

A plank it felt we walked.
They lifted the lid
right there and we filed
past like ants, bearing

twice our weight
in sorrow. It wasn't
true. That ain't you—
too grey, and serious,

right side of your face
fallen, cotton
filling your nose—
at least the suit looked new.

We held each other a long time
after and could not speak,
like you. Get up,
Stand up, we'll sing

later, the reggae you loved
your brother will strum
stumbling on a guitar, and for
a moment you'll be there, here,

where we'd been brought to visit
too late, like fools.
At the grave we step
past crumbling stones

and dead flowers to stand
on the red rise
of dirt already dug
for you. The sound

of them letting you down.
The sound of men scraping
and scraping what
I can't quite see, spreading

the cool concrete
over you by hand. And it takes
long, so long, like death—
like we once thought life.

The choir lifts us up
with their voices above
the coconut trees—*Habari
Jemba* they sing—

and the tune tells me Isn't That
Good News.
Cell phones chiming
their songs too.

After, we place white flowers
on your hardening tomb.
Is it only the sun
we shade our faces from?

Our sweat a thousand tears.

21 September

SABBATH [WAIT IN VAIN]

And all Sunday we slept

starting once
and then again
asleep, wake

only when it's dark.
It's one
in the night

Swahili time—
we've learned now
to wear our watches

upside down.
We want to see
your town—that you there

on the corner,
haggling
with God?

Later we'll sneak
& chew *tchat* in honor
of you, keeping you

hidden in our cheeks
for hours. You are
the Tusker

downed warm,
the chili sauce we sweat
our kingfish with,

fruit we don't dare touch.
Scrabble your fiancée's mother
always wins.

HOMESIT. HONEY-
ED. I want
to stay here

forever, or for you,
to see how happy
your life might

make me, us
left to live it
for you.

And tomorrow
back to the work
that is life, grief, what's

left: climbing
the church tower
till we can't go

any higher, creaking up
the spire past the bells
I want to ring

but it's too early.
Down again, we'll wait
in the churchyard & watch

children playing tag, taunting
whoever's it & pretending
safe. Walk on

down to a jetty
where men line up pissing
into the unmoved sea,

the shore rocking
a tide full of bottles
like wishes washed

back empty.

We decide the last

minute, day we are
        to leave, to fly for a tour

of Zanzibar—
        the prop plane pulling far

above the city and shore
        that you loved, leaving

the ground like bodies behind.
        Shadows of clouds

across green water.
        Whatever I fear,

a fall, does not happen, or has
        happened already—who can

say. You're gone.
        And the sun

pays no mind, still leaves
        the water blues and green

and colors I cannot name
        but imagine you always

had a word for. Stone Town
        itself is beautiful and loud

and lush, fish split open
        like mouths in the market, cats

waiting for what falls.
    The Joba Tree, tall—

where slaves once were tied and sold
    and whipped to show

how strong—
    long since chopped down.

Red marble
    in the chapel

built over the stump.
    Here, the House of Wonder

is mostly empty, a few rusty
    Communist cars—and at last we reach

ocean bare feet can feel,
    fruit you can peel

and trust. Nose full of dust.
    Today's never enough—

the flight back too quick
    while the pilot barely looks,

fills out forms and carbons.
    In sunset Dar es Salaam

spread out against the ocean
    like a hand.

You're gone.
    Below, drifting plumes

of smoke. Can it be
    too much to hope—

that tonight the sailboats
    will fill their wings

with wind and skim
    home quickly

across the sky of sea.

25 September

CATCH A FIRE

I arrive home to cyclones,
to trees broken like the heat
hasn't yet. Autumn
nowhere in sight except

a few leaves starting
their fall fire. Driving without
eyes for wreckage,
I don't notice right away—

Otis Redding sings A Change
Is Gonna Come and I sob
one last time you're gone.
High up, the BILLIONS

SOLD sign mangled,
once golden arches turned
almost an ampersand—
a few miles along it dawns

what storms I've missed.
Signs ripped down.
Roofs made only of tarp.
Pink tongues of insulation

pulled from the mouths
of houses now silent.
*Looking for a sign
from God?*

one billboard asks—
This is it.
What's left
of the Hillview Motel

no longer needs say
VACANCY.
Only the hill
still here. The corn

brown and shorn.
In a few weeks who can tell
what's being built
and what torn down—

flattened, the fields
all look the same. For now
this charcoal smell
fluttering past the hill—

It's been too hard living

And I'm afraid to die—
the thick smoke billowing
from burning
what's still green

but can't be saved.

25 September

REDEMPTION SONG

Finally fall.
At last the mist,
heat's haze, we woke
these past weeks with

has lifted. We find
ourselves chill, a briskness
we hug ourselves in.
Frost greying the ground.

Grief might be easy
if there wasn't still
such beauty—would be far
simpler if the silver

maple didn't thrust
its leaves into flame,
trusting that spring
will find it again.

All this might be easier if
there wasn't a song
still lifting us above it,
if wind didn't trouble

my mind like water.
I half expect to see you
fill the autumn air
like breath—

At night I sleep
on clenched fists.
Days I'm like the child
who on the playground

falls, crying
not so much from pain
as surprise.
I'm tired of tide

taking you away,
then back again—
what's worse, the forgetting
or the thing

you can't forget.
Neither yet—
last summer's
choir of crickets

grown quiet.

19 October

HYMN [SATISFY MY SOUL]

After the angels
After the arguments
over death and what's
after, after the water

has returned as rain
I will wander
till I am the water
washing me clean

After cold spell
After wind and weather
And me in my light coat
held closed against the breeze

After the knife of the wind
The trees growing
a skin you can see through
Icing over

After the river
After the cough and the leaves
that dance wide circles
The blood leaving the face

After we face the silence
What we never name
After repair
and the song of repair

After even heaven
What will we have then
After the after
I will still call you friend

22 September

EULOGY [PEOPLE GET READY]

And so the snow.

Far away the cactus flowering.

White morning making

my hands sting.

Lilies in a refrigerator

losing scent.

Tell me the weather

wherever you are.

Let snow send its angels—

lay down and wave

numb arms.

Deepening drifts.

We who are left

like mailboxes along a country road

huddle together in the cold

awaiting word.

5 December

ONE LOVE

Long ladder
        the rain makes

The thirsty
        throat of God—

The night of the day
we buried you
we sang every
Bob Marley song we knew

by heart or whatever
it was that kept
us up, and together—
call it *gut*—

It sure wasn't
legs that kept anyone
that day moving
numb.

A fork
        in the road like a tongue

Long night
        the heat makes—

The wide open mouth
of your brother's guitar
Your mother & us making music
to shut the silence

that is nowhere
but where

you might be, planted
beneath the palm trees.

We sway
      how long I cannot say

Long ladder
      of wished-for rain—

Later that night
we each sing some
song that is ours,
whatever we know—by gut—

& I sing the thing
that's kept me
company all day:
It's me It's me

It's me O Lord
      standing in the need

Of prayer—
      It's me It's me It's me—

O Lord—

Your fiancée tall
& sleepless
One brother strumming
One outside smoking

And another already
quiet under a hill.
The old song
my love sang:

From this valley they say
    you are going

We will miss your bright
    eyes & sweet smile—

Later your father
giving stories to the dawn
tells of his great-uncle
who lived to be

one hundred
twenty-two years old
& was still
going strong—

Know how he died?
    He took his own life

Left a note saying *God*
    has forgotten me.

It's me It's me
O Lord—
Tonight I
and I are afraid

we may have slipped
God's mind—
Above us
the stubbed-out stars

The dark unmoving
    mouth of the guitar—

Tonight, by gut,
I pray you are
God—
but not forgotten—

O earth
      of a thousand exits

O endless
endings—
Why does waiting
feel like pain

& pain waiting?
How to finish
this song,
say my goodbye—

Long ladder
      the days make

Short time
      to climb.

Spring 2003

COMMENCEMENT

Already the apartments
unfilling. Steady rain.
The feeling of rented

gowns against the skin.
Of rented everything.
That rain

again. The green—
loud sound of digging,
whine from a far-off machine.

Tornadoes take away
whole towns,
touching down. Families

try to find
each other, pointing out
their child in the crowd—

That one's mine,
proud. Teams practice
sliding home

dusting off uniforms
& somewhere the tailor is bored
to tears with nothing

left to hem. Rained
out games—
But the flowers love it

says the man selling me
sweet tea.
In my yard what I thought

were only weeds
turns out are really
a hundred tiny

blooming maple trees.

HOMAGE TO PHILLIS WHEATLEY

Poet & Servant to Mr. John Wheatley of Boston,
On Her Maiden Voyage to England

There are days I can understand
why you would want to board
broad back of some ship
and sail: venture, not homeward
but toward Civilization's

Cold seat,—having from wild
been stolen, and sent into more wild
of Columbia, our exiles
and Christians clamoring upon
the cobblestones of Bostontown—

Sail cross an Atlantic (this time) mild,
the ship's polite and consumptive
passengers proud. Your sickness
quit soon as you disembarked in mist
of London—free, finally, of our Republic's

Rough clime, its late converts who thought
they would not die, or die simply
in struggle, martyr to some God,—
you know of gods there
are many, who is really only

One—and that sleep, restless fever
would take most you loved. Why
fate fight? Death, dark mistress,
would come a-heralding silent
the streets,—no door to her closed,

No stair (servant, or front) too steep.
Even Gen. Washington, whom you praise,
victorious, knows this—will even admit
you to his parlor. Who could resist a Negress
who can recite Latin and speak the Queen's?

Docked among the fog and slight sun
of London, you know who you are not
but that is little new. Native
of nowhere—you'll stay a spell, return,
write, grow still. I wake with you

In my mind, leaning, learning
to write—your slight profile
that long pull of lower lip, its pout
proving you rescued by
some sadness too large to name.

My Most Excellence, my quill
and ink lady, you scrawl such script
no translation it needs—
your need is what's missing, unwritten
wish to cross back but not back

Into that land (for you) of the dead—
you want to see from above
deck the sea, to pluck from wind
a sense no Land can
give: drifting, looking not

For Leviathan's breath, nor for waves
made of tea, nor for mermen half
out of water (as you)—down
in the deep is not the narwhal enough real?
Beneath our wind-whipt banner you smile

At Sea which owns no country.

Notes

Thanks to a Guggenheim Foundation Fellowship and an NEA Literature Fellowship that allowed me to complete this book.

The title "Nicodemus," besides being an apocryphal book of the Bible, refers to an all-black settlement in western Kansas, the subject of a fine book *Exodusters*. The italicized epigraph is found on a poster from the postbellum period.

"Guernica" appeared in *The Progressive,* and is in memoriam June Jordan, who admired it after it was published.

"East Jesus" appeared in *Georgia Magazine* and is for Laura Wexler and Steve Lickteig.

"West Hell," "Guinea Gall," and "Prayer" also appeared in a piece commissioned by *Virginia Quarterly Review* to accompany paintings by Romare Bearden.

An earlier version of "Signs" appeared in *Sam Durant,* a catalog for the artist's Los Angeles MOCA retrospective.

"Incident," which tells one man's true story, takes its title from Countee Cullen's poem of the same name.

"Throne of the Third Heaven . . ." is the name of the altar made entirely of aluminum foil by self-taught artist James Hampton. Found in his garage after his death, Hampton's life work is now on view in the Smithsonian.

"Paradise Gardens" is the name of folk artist and preacher Howard Finster's sculpture garden near Rome, Georgia.

"For the Confederate Dead" appeared in *DoubleTake.*

"Lost Looking for Behavior Cemetery" is for Sean Hill.

"April in Paris" appeared in *Asheville Poetry Review.*

"Homage to Phillis Wheatley" appeared in *Paris Review,* and refers to the first black poet to publish a book in what soon would become the United States.

In the section "Americana," I began by attempting to write about a series of mythical towns, such as "Guinea Gall" and "West Hell," many of which are named in the folklore collected by Zora Neale Hurston. The rest of the places are real, or are real now.

"African Elegy" is for Philippe Wamba, friend and author, who was killed in a car accident in Kenya on the one-year anniversary of September 11th. He was thirty-one. Philippe had just returned to the African continent, where he'd grown up and where his father and family were from, after spending a number of years in the United States of his mother's birth. This dual African and African American heritage was the subject of his first book *Kinship;* he was conducting research for his second book, on contemporary Africa, when he died.

　　"African Elegy" is an account of learning of his death, attending his funeral in his home of Tanzania, and after. The poems take their titles in part from the Bob Marley songs and reggae Philippe loved. Besides being dedicated to the memory of Philippe, the poem and this book are also for the Wamba family, his fiancée, and his many friends, who all miss him terribly.

—KY

Permissions Acknowledgments

A Note About the Author

Kevin Young is the author of four previous collections of poetry and the editor of Library of America's *John Berryman: Selected Poems,* Everyman's Library Pocket Poets anthologies *Blues Poems* and *Jazz Poems,* and *Giant Steps: The New Generation of African American Writers.* His book *Jelly Roll* was a finalist for the National Book Award and the Los Angeles Times Book Prize, and won the Paterson Poetry Prize. The recent recipient of a Guggenheim fellowship and an NEA fellowship, Young is currently the Atticus Haygood Professor of English and Creative Writing and curator of the Raymond Danowski Poetry Library at Emory University in Atlanta, Georgia.

A Note on the Type

This book was set in Granjon, a type originally designed by George W. Jones, who based his drawings on a face used by Claude Garamond (ca. 1480–1561) in his beautiful French books. Granjon more closely resembles Garamond's own type than do any of the various modern faces that bear his name. It is named for Robert Granjon, a type cutter and printer active in Antwerp, Lyons, Rome, and Paris from 1523 to 1590. Granjon, the boldest and most original designer of his time, was one of the first to practice the trade of typefounder apart from that of printer.

Composed by Creative Graphics,
Allentown, Pennsylvania
Printed and bound by R. R. Donnelley & Sons,
Crawfordsville, Indiana
Designed by Anthea Lingeman